GIACOMO CARI

JEPHTE

(Jephthah)

Oratorio
for SATB soli,
SSSATB chorus,
optional strings without violas,
and organ continuo

revised and edited by

JANET BEAT

Order No: NOV 072302

NOVELLO PUBLISHING LIMITED

EDITORIAL NOTES

Sources

    A Paris, Bibliothèque nationale, MS Vm¹ 1.477. A single volume devoted to *Jephte* in the hand of Marc-Antoine Charpentier (d. 1704), a pupil of the composer.

    B loc. cit., MS Rés. F. 934a, pp. 1-62.

    C loc. cit., MS Vm¹ 1.475.

    D Versailles, Bibliothèque de Versailles, MS musicale 58, ff. 1-22.

    E Hamburg, Staats- und Universitätsbibliothek, MS MC/270 (41 ND VI 2425) pp. 115-46.

    F Oxford, Bodleian Library, MS MUS.SCH. c. 204 (vocal and instrumental parts in the hand of Edward Lowe, d. 1682).

    G loc. cit., MS MUS.SCH. c. 9, pp. 95-118.

    H Oxford, Christ Church, Music MS 37, ff. 1-22v.

    J loc. cit., Music MS 13, pp. 119-20 (final chorus only).

    K Kircheri (Athanasii), *Musurgia Universalis* (Rome, 1650), vol. 1, pp. 604-5 (final chorus only).

Beyond these there is a considerable number of English sources which, though interesting as testimony to the long-standing popularity of the work in this country, are of secondary value only.

Text

All these sources differ among themselves as to:

    (*i*) Small points of rhythm (♩. ♪ or ♪ ♪ ; ♩. ♪ or ♩ ♩ and so on), ties in the organ bass, verbal underlay, or treatment of anticipatory notes at cadences

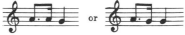

    (*ii*) The shape of the final chorus.

    (*iii*) The presence or absence of indications for string accompaniment.

    (*iv*) Ornamentation. Only one source (**D**) gives any indication of ornamentation, using the French sign +.

    (*v*) Bars 35 and 37.

All things considered, it seemed best to accept **A**, which, in the absence of an autograph, appears to stand in the most direct line from Carissimi, as the soundest basis of text. The few departures from it are mentioned in footnotes.

As to (*i*) above, no useful purpose would be served by a collation of all these matters; but they indicate that some freedom may legitimately be claimed in the delivery of declamatory monody.

As to (*ii*), sources **F** (vocal parts) and **H** have a shorter version than **A**, while **F** (instrumental parts) and **G** have a longer one. It happens that the longer version was included by Chrysander in his edition (*Carissimi's Werke . . . erste Abtheilung*). He appears to have worked from sources at Hamburg; yet this longer version is not found in **E**. It seems, however, that two other Hamburg MSS of the work were destroyed during World War II, and one can only suppose that Chrysander took these bars from one or other of these now lost MSS, which may be postulated as a 'ghost' source supporting the longer version. Its authority cannot be precisely determined; the bars involved, not found in **A**, are here printed in small size notes for the benefit of those who prefer to use them.

As to (*iii*), it appears that this oratorio was intended to be performed with organ accompaniment only. However, parts for Violins I and II and Cello-bass, derived from voice parts and the basso continuo, are provided in **D** and **F** for all choruses save 'Abiit ergo'. For those who wish to use them, such parts are available in connection with this edition. The violin parts are marked in the vocal score; whenever the violins play, the cello-bass has a part extracted from the bass voice and basso continuo parts.

(*v*) concerns an important difference between sources **A** and **D** on the one hand and **B C E F G H** on the other as to the basso continuo in bars 35 and 37. **D** agrees with **A** as amended, where the others read *f, g, f, d* quavers (bar 35, 3rd and 4th beats) and *c, d, c, A* quavers (bar 37, 1st and 2nd beats).

For a detailed discussion of (*ii*) and (*iii*), see my paper 'Two problems in Carissimi's *Jephte*', *The Music Review*, August-November 1973.

Editorial Procedure

Note values and the 3/2 time-signature remain unchanged, but the modern 4/4 signature has been substituted for C. The naming of voice parts is editorial. Those for Jephte and Filia are in the tenor and soprano C clefs in the source. Other original clefs, where different from those now used, are shown here on preliminary staves. Crossed ties and shakes in square brackets are editorial. The ornament sign + found in **D** has been rendered as *w* or *tr* according to context. Suggested metronome marks, dynamics, and style have been entered in the keyboard part to the choruses and arioso passages. A purely editorial accidental is enclosed in square brackets, while all cancelling accidentals in the modern convention are printed in small size. In the organ part the L.H. notes strictly follow the basso continuo of the source-text, while the R.H. notes are editorial.

Performance

At the longer cadence notes marked with a shake the soloist should feel free to introduce some individual degree of ornamentation. The declamatory solo work (Historicus, Jephte, Filia) should be delivered dramatically and with intense feeling, not in any 'religioso' style. The organ continuo part here provided is deliberately of only a simple, basic character, which the player should adapt (especially as to timing, and reiteration of harmonies) in accordance with the singers' requirements.

J.E.B. 1974

String parts are available on hire, conductor using the vocal score.

DURATION **28** MINUTES

HISTORICUS
Cum vocasset in proelium filios Israel rex filiorum Ammon, et verbis Jephte acquiescere noluisset, factus est super Jephte Spiritus Domini, et progressus ad filios Ammon votum vovit Domini dicens:

When the king of the children of Ammon made war against the children of Israel, and hearkened not unto the words of Jephthah, then there came upon Jephthah the Spirit of the Lord, and he went up against the children of Ammon and vowed unto the Lord, saying:

JEPHTE
Si tradiderit Dominus filios Ammon in manus meas, quicumque primus de domo mea occurrerit mihi, offeram illum Domino in holocaustum.

If thou shalt indeed deliver the children of Ammon into my hands, whatsoever first cometh forth of the doors of my house to meet me, I will offer to the Lord for a burnt offering.

CHORUS
Transivit ergo Jephte ad filios Ammon, ut in spiritu forti et virtute Domini pugnaret contra eos.

Then Jephthah passed over to the children of Ammon, and he fought in the spirit and the strength of God against them.

DUET
Et clangebant tubae, et personabant tympana, et proelium commissum est adversus Ammon.

And the trumpets sounded, and the drums were beaten, when battle was joined against the children of Ammon.

BASS SOLO
Fugite, cedite, impii, perite gentes, occumbite in gladio; Dominus exercituum in proelium surrexit, et pugnat contra vos.

Flee from us, yield to us, impious ones, give away, ye heathen, and fall before our mighty sword; for the God of Israel is risen up to battle and fights against our foes.

CHORUS
Fugite, cedite, impii, corruite, et in furore gladii dissipamini.

Flee from us, yield to us, impious ones, we scatter you, and with our keen and glittering swords we hew you down.

HISTORICUS
Et percussit Jephte viginti civitates Ammon plaga magna nimis.

Jephthah therefore smote them, and took from them twenty cities, and there was a grievous slaughter.

TRIO
Et ululantes filii Ammon, facti sunt coram filiis Israel humiliati.

And he subdued the children of Ammon, for the Lord delivered them to the children of Israel.

HISTORICUS
Cum autem victor Jephte in domum suam reverteretur, occurrens ei unigenita filia sua cum tympanis et choris praecinebat:

And Jephthah came to Mispeh unto his house when he returned, and behold, there came forth his only daughter to meet him with timbrels and with dances, and she sang thus:

FILIA
Incipite in tympanis et psallite in cymbalis. Hymnum cantemus Domino, et modulemur canticum. Laudemus regem coelitum, laudemus belli principem, qui filiorum Israel victorem ducem reddidit.

Come, strike the merry timbrels and sound the joyful cymbals. Let us sing praises unto the Lord, and. let us magnify his name, yea, let us praise the God of heaven and magnify the mighty King who doth restore the conquering leader of the children of Israel.

DUET
Hymnum cantemus Domino, et modulemur canticum, qui dedit nobis gloriam et Israel victoriam.

Sing unto the Lord, and offer hymns to him who giveth us the glory and Israel the victory.

FILIA
Cantate mecum Domino, cantate omnes populi, laudate belli principem, qui nobis dedit gloriam et Israel victoriam.

Sing to the Lord with me, sing praises, all ye peoples, to the mighty King who giveth us the glory and Israel the victory.

CHORUS
Cantemus omnes Domino, laudemus belli principem qui dedit nobis gloriam et Israel victoriam.

Let us sing unto the Lord and praise the mighty King who giveth us the glory and Israel the victory.

HISTORICUS
Cum vidisset Jephte, qui votum Domino voverat, filiam suam venientem in occursum, in dolore et lachrimis scidit vestimenta sua et ait:

And it came to pass, when Jephthah saw his only daughter, his well-beloved, coming forth to meet him, he remembered his vow to God, and he rent his garments and spake thus:

JEPHTE
Heu mihi! filia mea, heu decepisti me, filia unigenita, et tu pariter, heu filia mea decepta es.

Woe is me! Alas! my daughter, thou hast undone me, thou, my only daughter; and thou, likewise, my daughter, art undone.

FILIA
Cur ego te pater decepi, et cur ego filia tua unigenita decepta sum?

How have I, O my father, undone thee, and how am I, thy only daughter, undone?

JEPHTE
Aperui os meum ad Dominum, ut quicumque primus de domo mea occurrerit mihi offeram illum Domino in holocaustum. Heu mihi! filia mea, heu decepisti me, filia unigenita, decepisti me, et tu pariter, heu filia mea, decepta es.

I have opened my mouth to the Lord that whatsoever first cometh forth of the doors of my house to meet me, I will offer to the Lord for a burnt offering. Alas! my daughter, thou hast undone me, thou, my only daughter, and thou likewise, my daughter, thou art undone.

FILIA
Pater mi, si vovisti votum Domino reversus victor ab hostibus, ecce ego, filia tua unigenita, offer me in holocaustum victoriae tuae, hoc solum pater mi praesta filiae tuae unigenitae ante quam moriar.

O my father, thou hast opened thy mouth to the Lord and hast returned to thy house victorious, therefore do to me according to thy vow, offer me for a burnt offering before the Lord, but this thing, O my father, grant to me, thy only beloved daughter, before I die.

JEPHTE
Quid poterit animam tuam, quid poterit te, moritura filia, consolari?

But what can give thee consolation, yea, what can give thee, my unhappy daughter, consolation?

FILIA
Dimitte me, ut duobus mensibus circumeam montes, ut cum sodalibus meis, plangam virginitatem meam.

O let me go, that for two months I may wander upon the mountains with my companions, bewailing my virginity.

JEPHTE

Vade, filia mea unigenita, et plange virginitatem tuam.

Go, my only beloved daughter, go and bewail thy virginity.

CHORUS

Abiit ergo in montes filia Jephte, et plorabat cum sodalibus virginitatem suam, dicens:

Then went the daughter of Jephthah unto the mountains and bewailed her virginity, herself and her companions, saying:

FILIA

Plorate colles, dolete montes, et in afflictione cordis mei ululate! [Echo: *ululate!*] Ecce moriar virgo et non potero morte mea meis filiis consolari, ingemiscite silvae, fontes et flumina, in interitu virginis lachrimate! [Echo: *lachrimate!*] Heu me dolentem in laetitia populi, in victoria Israel et gloria patris mei, ego, sine filiis virgo, ego, filia unigenita, moriar et non vivam. Exhorrescite, rupes, obstupescite, colles, valles, et cavernae, in sonitu horribili resonate! [Echo: *resonate!*]
Plorate, filii Israel, plorate virginitatem meam, et Jephte filiam unigenitam in carmine doloris lamentamini.

Lament, ye valleys, bewail, ye mountains, and in the affliction of my heart be ye afflicted! [Echo: be ye afflicted!] Lo! I shall die a virgin and shall not in my death find consolation in my children. Then bemoan me, ye woods and fountains and rivers, make lamentation for the death of a virgin. [Echo: make lamentation!] See, while the people rejoice I am mourning in the victory of Israel, in the glory of my father, I, in my virginity childless, I, an only beloved daughter, must die and no longer live. Then tremble, ye rocks, be astonished, ye mountains, valleys and caves, resound with horror and fearfulness! [Echo: be resounding!] Weep, ye children of Israel, weep for a hapless virgin, and lament for Jephthah's only daughter with songs of sadness.

CHORUS

Plorate, filii Israel, plorate, omnes virgines, et filiam Jephte unigenitam in carmine doloris lamentamini.

Weep, ye children of Israel, weep, O all ye maidens, and lament for Jephthah's only daughter with songs of sadness.

Translation after John Troutbeck

STRING PARTS AVAILABLE ON HIRE

JEPHTE
(Jephthah)

Revised and edited by
Janet Beat

GIACOMO CARISSIMI

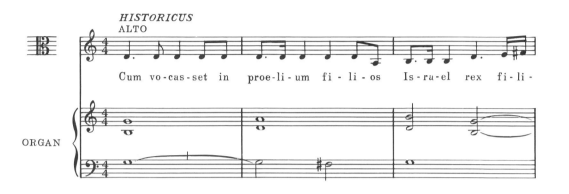

gres-sus ad fi - li - os Am-mon vo-tum vo-vit Do - mi - ni di - cens:

10

JEPHTE
TENOR

Si tra - di - de - rit Do - mi - nus fi - li - os Am-mon in man-us me - as,

14

qui - cum - que pri - mus de do - mo me - a oc - cur - re - rit mi - hi,

17

of - fe - ram il - lum Do - mi - no in ho - lo - cau - stum.

19

CHORUS

1) Bar 23, Soprano III. ♩• ♪ in A

2) Bar 27, Bass. ♩• ♪ in A

20076

3) Bar 35, Continuo in **A** reads [notation] but Charpentier has written beneath it the version here given with the legend 'Caris.' (? Carissimi).

4) Bar 37, Continuo in **A** reads [notation] but again Charpentier has written beneath it the version here given with the same legend.

6

BASS SOLO

Fu - gi-te, fu-gi-te, ce - di-te, ce - di-te, im - pi - i, ce - di-te,

♩=80

f vigorously

42   7 6

ce - di-te, im - pi - i, pe - ri-te gen - tes, pe - ri-te gen - tes, oc -

44   7 6   7 6   7 6

cum-bi-te, oc-cum-bi-te in gla - - - di - o;

47

Do-mi-nus ex-er-ci-tu-um in proe-li-um sur-rex-it, in proe-li-um sur-rex-it, et

50   #

5) Bar 52, Bass in A reads

ut pug-nar-et con-tra _____ vos, ut pug-nar-et con-

tra _____ vos, ut pug-nar-et con-tra vos, pug - nar-et con - tra vos.

20076

pug-nat con-tra vos, ———————— et pug-nat con-tra vos, ———————— et

53

pug-nat con-tra vos, et pug - - nat con - tra vos.

56

CHORUS

S I

Fu - gi - te, fu - gi - te, ce - di - te, ce - di - te, im - pi - i, fu - gi - te, fu - gi - te,

S II

Fu - gi - te, fu - gi - te, ce - di - te, ce - di - te, im - pi - i, fu - gi - te, fu - gi - te,

S III

Fu - gi - te, fu - gi - te, ce - di - te, ce - di - te, im - pi - i, fu - gi - te, fu - gi - te,

A

Fu - gi - te, fu - gi - te,

T

Fu - gi - te, fu - gi - te,

B

Fu - gi - te, fu - gi - te,

59

6) Bar 59, Soprano III. in A

7) Bar 60, Soprano II.⎫
   Bar 61, Tenor.   ⎬ in A

20076

8) Bar 62, Soprano III. ♪♪ in A

20076

* Bars 70-71. There is much to be said for taking this organ bass an octave higher.

20076

HISTORICUS
SOPRANO

Et per-cus-sit Jeph-te vi-gin-ti ci-vi-ta-tes Am-mon pla-ga mag-na, pla-ga mag-na ni - mis.

TRIO (a few voices only)
SI

Et u-lu-lan-tes fi-li-i Am-mon,

SII

Et u-lu-lan-tes fi-li-i Am - mon, fac-ti

A

Et u-lu-lan-tes fi-li-i Am - mon, fac-ti

♩ = 66

fac - ti sunt co-ram fi-li-is Is-ra-el hu - mi-li-a - ti.

sunt co-ram fi-li-is Is - - ra-el hu-mi-li - a - ti.

sunt co-ram fi-li-is Is - ra - el hu - mi-li-a - ti.

*Bars 78-88. There is much to be said for taking this organ bass an octave higher.

20076

14

20076

9) Bar 167, Soprano II. ♩ ♩ in A

✱ Bars 169-171. There is much to be said for taking this organ bass an octave higher, as **D** in fact does.

* Bars 174-176. There is much to be said for taking this organ bass an octave higher.

20076

18

20

20076

20076

22

vic-tor ab hos - ti - bus, ec - ce e - go, fi-li-a tu-a u-ni - ge-ni-ta, of-fer

244

me in ho-lo-cau-stum vic - to - ri-ae tu - ae, hoc so-lum pa-ter

248

mi praes-ta fi-li-ae tu-ae u-ni-ge-ni-tae an - te quam mo - ri - ar.

252

JEPHTE

Quid po - te-rit a - ni-mam tu - am, quid po - te-rit te, mo-ri-tu-ra

256

24

20076

sil-vae, fon-tes et flu-mi-na, in in-te-ri-tu vir-gi-nis la-chri-ma-

305

-te, fon-tes et flu-mi-na, in in-te-ri-tu vir-gi-nis la-chri-ma-

309   4 3   ♭5   ♭   ♭6   6

-te!   Heu me do-len-tem,   heu

SI (a few voices only)

la - chri-ma - te!

SII (a few voices only)

la-chri-ma - te!

pp

313   4 3   ♭6   6   6 5   ♯
                          4 3

me do-len-tem   in lae-ti-ti-a po - pu-li,   in vic-to-ri-a Is - ra-el et

318

32

379

383b

10) Bar 381, Soprano III, Alto. in A

11) There is some doubt about the authenticity of bars 383b - 394, which are found only in source F, possibly supported by a 'ghost' source. See Introduction.

389

395

Printed and bound in Great Britain by
Caligraving Limited Thetford Norfolk

EARLY CHORAL MUSIC

BONONCINI, Antonio
ed Peter Smith
STABAT MATER
For SATB soli, SATB chorus, strings and organ

BONONCINI, Giovanni
ed Anthony Ford
WHEN SAUL WAS KING
For SAT soli, SATB chorus, strings and organ continuo, with optional parts for two oboes and bassoon

GABRIELI, Giovanni
ed Denis Stevens
IN ECCLESIIS
For SATB soli, SATB chorus, instruments and organ

LASSUS, Orlandus
ed Clive Wearing
STABAT MATER
For unaccompanied double choir (SSAT, ATTB)

MONTEVERDI, Claudio
ed John Steele
BEATUS VIR
For SSATTB chorus, instruments and organ continuo

PALESTRINA, da Giovanni
ed W Barclay Squire
STABAT MATER
For unaccompanied double choir (SATB, SATB)

RIGATTI, Giovanni Antonio
ed Jerome Roche
CONFITEBOR TIBI
For SSAATTB chorus, instruments and organ continuo

SCARLATTI, Alessandro
ed John Steele
AUDI FILIA
For SSA soli, SSATB chorus, instruments, string orchestra and organ
ed John Steele
DIXIT DOMINUS
For SATB soli, SATB chorus, strings and organ continuo
ed John Steele
ST CECILIA MASS
For SSATB soli, SATB chorus, strings and organ continuo

VALLS, Francisco
MISSA SCALA ARETINA
For 11 voices in 3 choirs (SAT, SSAT, SATB), orchestra with organ continuo

VARIOUS
TEN RENAISSANCE DIALOGUES
For unaccompanied mixed voices by Lassus, Gabrieli, Morley and others